Also by Stephen Oliver

Henwise (1975)
& interviews (1978)
Autumn Songs (1978)
Letter To James K. Baxter (1980)
Earthbound Mirrors (1984)
Guardians, Not Angels (1993)
Islands of Wilderness—A Romance (1996)
Unmanned (1999)
Election Year Blues (1999)
Night of Warehouses: Poems 1978–2000 (2001)
Deadly Pollen (2003)
Ballads, Satire & Salt—A Book of Diversions (2003)
Either Side The Horizon (2005)
Parable Of The Sea Sponge (2007)
Harmonic (2008)
Apocrypha (2010)
Intercolonial (2013)
Gone: Satirical Poems: New & Selected (2016)
Luxembourg (2018)
Heroides / 15 Sonnets (2020)

THE SONG OF GLOBULE
80 Sonnets

STEPHEN OLIVER

GP
GREYWACKE PRESS
Lat. 25°/50° South. Long. 145°/180° East

First Published 2020

Greywacke Press
9 Lynch St
Hughes
ACT 2605
Australia
reid1801@bigpond.com   greywackepress@gmail.com

Oliver, Stephen, 1950-
Title: *The Song Of Globule*
ISBN   9 780646 812144

Cover design/photo: Stephen Oliver

Especial thanks to Amy Tonkin (cover) and John Denny (internals) for their generous InDesign work on this book.

Old entrance to the iconic Olympia Milk Bar, revealed after the demolition of the Stanmore Cinema on Parramatta Road, Sydney, September 2001.

Sydney Tower by Stephen Oliver created in 1995 and later designed as a text-based art poster 111.5 x 40 cm for 2000 but never released.

Heroides / 15 Sonnets (Nos: 64-78) first published as a self-contained chapbook by Puriri Press, Auckland 2020.

A catalogue record for this book is available from the
National Library of Australia

© Stephen Oliver

All rights reserved.
No part of this publication may be reproduced, stored in a retrieval system, or transmitted in any form or by any means, electronic, mechanical, photocopying, scanning, recording or otherwise, without the prior permission of the copyright owner.

Contents

The Song of Globule

1. escape from Eden — 3
2. life's a dirty job — 4
3. bad boys & grungy bars — 5
4. southerly buster — 6
5. 'Hey True Blue' — 7
6. 'mirror, mirror on the wall' — 8
7. a bridge too far — 9
8. passed by a billboard — 10
9. siren song — 11
10. wormhole — 12
11. ain't that the truth — 13
12. thick as pig shit — 14
13. at a premium — 15
14. burst like an aerial shell — 16
15. this goose-stepping bird — 17
16. an enclosed garden — 18
17. more a hard grind — 19
18. Sydney's oldest bones — 20
19. ceiling fans susurrated — 21
20. primal gardens — 22
21. where on this motley map — 23
22. a fish on the hook — 24
23. micky finned — 25
24. womby vaultage — 26
25. cities are whorehouses — 27
26. Headlands Hotel — 28
27. an inch of daylight — 29

28. scattered husks   30
29. an oyster shell galaxy   31
30. the promise of falsehood   32
31. half stonkered   33
32. Hellenic Bakery   34
33. takes all sorts   35
34. 'with unhurrying chase'   36
35. outside of time   37
36. Jesus hobo   38
37. nereid of the waves   39
38. that which haunts   40
39. a dream of Sorrento   41
40. egalité   42
41. crimson bruise   43
42. Olympia Milk Bar   44
43. this harlot saint   45
44. act of defiance   46
45. Mt. Athos   47
46. before shunters   48
47. so long   49
48. O Sirius   50
49. Sophie Scholl   51
50. hillock of her hip   52
51. loop   53
52. bad mistake   54
53. generations   55
54. Thecla   56
55. never look back   57
56. twilight bat   58

57. yet retain a hold 59
58. tiny nails 60
59. techies and hipsters 61
60. slow blur 62
61. oikoumene 63
62. passed her by 64
63. hearts that harden 65
64. Penelope to Ulysses / I 66
65. Phyllis to Demophoon / ii 67
66. Briseis to Achilles / iii 68
67. Phaedra to Hippolytus / iv 69
68. Oenone to Paris / v 70
69. Hypsipyle to Jason / vi 71
70. Dido to Aeneas / vii 72
71. Hermione to Orestes / viii 73
72. Deianira to Hercules / ix 74
73. Ariadne to Theseus / x 75
74. Canace to Macareus / xi 76
75. Medea to Jason / xii 77
76. Laodamia to Protesilaus / xiii 78
77. Hypermnestra to Lynceus / xiv 79
78. Sappho to Phaon / xv 80
79. no oracles 81
80. follow the rails 82

Notes i-xiv

THE SONG OF GLOBULE

Why, from silvery peach-bloom,
From that shallow-silvery wine-glass on a short stem
This rolling, dropping, heavy globule?

Peach—D.H. Lawrence

1. *escape from Eden*

We could not leave the garden, we only
dreamed sin, and so we came to believe it.
One tumescent red apple brought us grief.
Old snake sidled through the night like a thief.
Cough. Slough. Was the ancient coat an ill fit?
She bought it, though knew he was a phony.
A stroppy full moon throttled the garden;
trees with no names danced amongst waterfalls
and glistened, way before the fall, shadows
gathered in sooty flocks amongst meadows.
God stomped and snorted in heavenly halls,
'*I condemn them to life without pardon.*'

Did Globule sprout seraphic wings for flight?
not beneath this bumpy sky—not tonight.

2. *life's a dirty job*

Pheromones hornily filled her blood tree,
spilling overnight from puberty's font.
Back of a Ford, Brad popped her cherry—O
Yay! to dumb girlhood she bid cheerio.
She quickly sussed that boys fancy a bonk,
so—safe-guarded her 'private property.'
She learnt. She grew up. But what did she fish
for from life's prickly pond, was she happy?
Life doesn't give a rat's arse how we feel.
We nose-balance our hopes much like a seal;
dreams may be free but some turn out crappy.
So Globule learnt that life is a mixed dish.

She found it best to live for the moment,
what could anyone gain from postponement?

3. *bad boys & grungy bars*

A sun bungee jumped the hours of the day
over the back fence of her North Shore home.
The city shone bright as a bracelet 'cross
the harbour's makeshift waves of fairy floss.
She niggled and nudged at her comfort zone,
the harbour bridge arched, a grey bird of prey.
Her chartered accountant father (poor sod)
and her smiley, house-proud, aproned mother,
took it for granted she would marry the
boy next-door—or next-door to him, maybe—
did not doubt the books balanced her future,
but she fancied that dude with the hot rod.

She'd take City Rail to the Inner West,
Newtown bad boys and grungy bars, the best!

4. *southerly buster*

A truck axle up-ended and upright
in a cloud collision stands Centre Point,
slapped up poster proud over the city,
battered, buffeted, lightning struck—ugly;
brassy as the town it's meant to anoint,
would be missed if it vanished overnight;
—fifty-six cables anchor the Tower—
which, if tied one to another, would reach
all the way from Sydney to Alice Springs.
As wind in the rigging of a ship sings,
would those cables twang along city streets
in a wind stretched, southerly buster hour?

Under this giant crow's nest in the food hall,
munching on a big burger, sat Globule.

5.   'Hey True Blue'

Her pal Jade tweeted, 'let's go out, be seen,
meet you like some place in the CBD.'
David Jones bright with heavenly spangle;
tight jeans, buckle belt, boots, tank top, bangle.
A train over the bridge from North Sydney,
the harbour sheen like a computer screen.
The third floor, window-peering mono-rail
warped on by like some bent polio brace,
strapped tightly around the city's kneecaps.
She feared the thing might suddenly collapse;
no way José! She put on her bright face.
The harbour grey-blue and cluttered with sail.

Strand Arcade. She decided to cut through,
flicked a coin. A busker sang, 'Hey True Blue.'

6. *'mirror, mirror on the wall'*

Famous for Nothing like Paris Hilton.
(No thanks) could anything ever phase her
in this prankster life that fled down the days
of her endless youth? Often, she did gaze
into the bathroom mirror's drippy blur,
hoping for—some sort of revelation—
(not likely) the word meant one fat zero.
A face stared back impassive. Goat-grey eyes,
half-surprised at, whatever, nothing much.
Her face, friendly as—in the mirror's clutch,
hungered for a grip on life, love and lies.
Just one more girl in search of some hero.

She sat on the stoop by the old wood shed,
then painted her toenails a fire truck red.

7. *a bridge too far*

Cyclists in a row peddled, lycra-lit,
left to right, into view, then out of sight,
wheels flurried, sped uniformly by, *whoosh!*
Upon Macquarie's Chair she parked her tush.
The harbour flared up acetylene white.
She had just given her boyfriend the flick.
Over the Botanic Gardens birds screeched;
sulphur-crested cockatoo—currawong.
She had met this dick at the Marble Bar,
finding 'normal' just seemed a bridge too far.
Another Friday night, what could go wrong,
as she tried to forget what her mom preached?

She watched a dog leap, to catch a Frisbee,
'So desperate to please,' she thought, 'like me.'

8. *passed by a billboard*

Again—inner city rail, 'red rattler'
blitzed another appointment, 'So I'm late.'
Like, as if she truly wanted the job;
working the phones for a few measly bob,
bugger that! She had enough on her plate,
still lived amongst the family clatter,
and paid minimal rent, but she was bored.
Yet what did she wish for—if anything,
she passed by a billboard: 'Be All You Can.
God Is Our Endgame. Get With His Program.'
Did she hear the celestial choir sing,
would she go to Niger, work for the Lord?

No way a poncy cleric as her boss,
better some job at Barons in The Cross.

9. *siren song*

Fort Denison's Martello tower sat
squat upon its rock, in middle harbour.
Handfuls of sudsy cloud drifted piecemeal
above the bridge, a half-sunk waterwheel
that churned the lazy day bluely over.
Out west, dully sounded a thunder clap.
Her friend Jade was only a tweet away;
the town sang its eternal siren song—
of that seductive choir she played her part,
swayed to the rhythm of the city's heart.
While the brassy sun beat its summer gong
golden bodies shimmered in every bay.

A bus to Bondi (the weather said fine),
though first she must wax her bikini line.

10. *wormhole*

That was the exoplanet in her dream,
the habitable zone, through the wormhole
back to Eden—she never looked so hot.
Youth and beauty were her eternal lot,
until she challenged divine protocol
and nakedness became something obscene.
Eden withered, turned into the Badlands;
gulches, ravines, canyons, an arid place.
The slate wiped clean, memory erased, gone.
What was once dream became evolution;
a beginning, middle, end to the race.
Globule concluded, why make any plans?

So she failed to seduce God, tough luck Eve,
hotly pursued by Adam—took her leave.

11. *ain't that the truth*

Evolution stopped at the door of God,
who asked, 'Had enough?' Regress to Eden.
Not even memory can drag us back,
a hope too far by half, the world's our rack.
Such is destiny, it can't be undone;
life-broth bubbling upon the earthly hob.
Globule advanced her girlhood with makeup,
foundation, lippy, her hair refulgent,
caught like a rabbit in the glare of youth.
That beauty doesn't last, ain't that the truth;
live for the moment, be self-indulgent—
though she would not evolve past a c-cup.

A mud-flat moon fingered a flounder, flop!
Life's what you make of it; it's all you've got.

12. *thick as pig shit*

Tamarama thrashed laundry loud. O spring.
Globule reclined languid upon her bed,
bored—considered doing a tumble wash,
flimsy cotton panties, thongs, bra, oh gosh!
wished for 'throw-away' underwear instead.
Hey nonny! Love is but a fickle thing.
She wants a kid or two, he wants to surf,
all that oxygen—yet thick as pig shit.
Great bodies both though not a brain between,
looking good out there is living the dream,
follow the fads, diets—and keeping fit.
'Fuck the fantasies', that's it, 'why not Perth?'

A thought struck hard as a knock at the door,
bucks are far better than boyfriends—for sure!

13. *at a premium*

Okay, Globule was no longer a teen
watching gulls circle off Circular Quay,
some kid at play in school and public park,
boisterous tomboy—happy as a lark.
Bygone days. O photoshopped memory,
moonrise brightly lit as a smartphone screen.
Nevertheless, she knew herself quite well,
reaction meant, more or less, attraction;
be in the moment, never let it go,
for long as it lasted (like) with some Joe.
To give the flick was simple subtraction—
just deleting his number from her cell.

Night clubby boys bedecked as cherubim,
told her straight guys are at a premium.

14. *burst like an aerial shell*

Globule celebrated fireworks as planned
glissading fan-like off the harbour bridge.
Puffballs of leery light *whizz! crackle! pop!*
Away from the CBD crowds atop
Bay View Crescent, she found a grassy ridge
to see the town turn into Disneyland.
The sky rained down bits of colour pell-mell,
Rozelle Bay blurred to a painter's palette.
Nearby, a party roared amidst the blear
of traffic horns welcoming in New Year.
She'd stay sober just for the hell of it,
meanwhile, sky-burst like an aerial shell.

City bells tolled as the midnight hour struck,
whole galaxies swirled in one clusterfuck.

15. *this goose-stepping bird*

It was peaceful in this Inner West park
no bigger than a pocket handkerchief,
on a swing with metal chains, wooden seat,
some out-of-the-way suburban back street,
a few bottle brush trees to give relief;
though her mood was not discernibly dark.
A myna bird strutting its stuff nearby
amongst the stubbies from the night before,
the cigarette butts and the bottle tops,
cocks its bandit head at her, and then stops—
this goose-stepping bird, nazi and outlaw.
Irked, she grabbed at a beer can and let fly.

An apartment block. A ranch slider slid.
The black cat jumped off the garbage tin lid.

16. *an enclosed garden*

I am that little girl upon the swing
flung from trough-to-crest airily skyward,
kicking cloud over treetops behind me
white as wave caps on a wind waffled sea.
Each hour is a newly dug treasure hoard
that rolls on like an endless ball of string.
Terracotta tiles, gooseneck finial,
barrel terrace, red brick apartment block,
granny flat and laneway, green wheelie bins,
scattered refuse—the discarded syringe;
my childhood is a backward running clock.
Upon the swing I am that little girl.

St Joseph's School and the presbytery,
an enclosed garden, a gnarled grapefruit tree.

17. *more a hard grind*

Hanging close by the Coronation Hall
with the Subud dudes doing what they do,
some kind of weird meditation, she thought.
The windows of the Courthouse Hotel caught
sunlight in baubles (she had had a few),
as warbled patterns formed on the pub wall.
City Rail scraped out of Newtown Station,
a Boeing scuffed off suburban rooftops
so low you could read Dunlop on the tyres,
its fuselage scribbled on by church spires.
Here in the Inner West she'd learned her chops,
though more a hard grind than revelation.

The Subud dudes were kicking up a storm,
an old codger placed a bet, checked the form.

18. Sydney's oldest bones

Watering hole for the local cop shop,
a pack of them claimed one end of the bar.
One bent copper's just as bent as the next,
stolid, stony-faced, stupidly perplexed.
A better pub than most around by far;
was Globule's occasional schooner stop.
Then, maybe, Camperdown Cemetery,
strolling by the giant Moreton Bay Fig
of St Stephen's Church, historic tombstones,
resting place for the city's oldest bones.
She'd find some shady spot to light a cig—
within this walled enclosure's greenery.

A sandstone angel on a stele blew
his trumpet into the whisp'ring bamboo.

19. *ceiling fans susurrated*

Ku-ring-gai Chase National Park in flame
over the Hawkesbury, the horizon
jumped up orange under ember attack.
Ash blanketed Hornsby Shire, furnace black,
out across the Inner West postal zone—
the cops claimed an arsonist was to blame.
The public bar TV flared siren red
with regular updates from the fire front,
ceiling fans susurrated—folk sipped beer,
one feigned interest, others didn't care;
the locals played pool, a few took a punt,
or stalwartly played at pokies, instead.

The jukebox rasped with a leathery throat,
'she gone with the man in the long black coat'.

20. *primal gardens*

Dreams devolved into a nocturnal sport,
as if something else, or other called out—
'for where the mind is there is the treasure'
something beyond all value or measure,
though what did it mean, what was this about?
You might say she had little to report.
Or could it be that Mary Magdalene
walked the primal gardens of her vision,
this shadow figure, a few seated men
gathered under a palm by some sheep pen.
Tattered cloud at dusk in soft collision,
words she imparted received with disdain.

Yet deep within Globule's murkiest dreams,
Lilith whispered, 'All is not what it seems.'

21. *where on this motley map*

The mirror parodied her gaze, bitchfaced,
no Furies to be had there, succubus—
absent; but mostly, she just felt 'sicked out,'
her face, expressionless, conjured a pout.
She felt not so much dull as querulous,
sat, scissor-crossed her legs, got up and paced.
Wherever she looked adventure beckoned;
autumn arrived with its rustling poplars.
But where on this motley map should she go,
maybe just throw a dart and make it so?
Oh, to chill on a Belize beach, topless.
A one-way ticket, get out—she reckoned.

Would she end up in Macau and languish,
to relinquish her English for Chinglish?

22. *a fish on the hook*

So, Globule dismissed the fantasy thing,
real life beckoned beyond the chat room;
forum or facebook buddies signalled naught,
any little kindness would sort it out
real time and—like a witch on a broom,
made her escape from that cybersex fling.
Yet, most likely gossip would pull her back,
and reel her in like a fish on the hook.
The laptop screen transmitted its phony
siren song, for hours, Globule sat lonely—
the world for her was an unread e-book;
she gazed deep into the pool of her Mac.

The moon rose with an inquisitive eye,
and fruit bats clicked by on the velvet sky.

23. *mickey finned*

Saturday afternoon, the Rose Hotel,
Erskineville, a favourite thing to do.
The public oval bar—live music scene,
tables on the pavement, seen-to-be-seen.
The minutes wore away, she downed a few;
'O solitude! If I must with thee dwell,'
floated into her head from old school days.
It was as if noises around her dimmed
for a moment, and objects grew brighter,
her vision sharpened, her head felt lighter.
OMG maybe she'd been mickey finned?
A glass deflected the setting sun's rays.

Yet, she could at will sit still as a book,
for to meditate was to see—not look.

24. *womby vaultage*

She sat. Saturday spun like a glass prism.
Ofttimes she sought a quiet place and found
the womby vaultage of some cathedral;
St Mary's via Hyde Park (when not full),
the scent of stale incense on sacred ground.
But this had nought to do with theism,
her moods were a pantheon of the gods.
Something she sensed or did not understand,
this monthly rebellion of the hormones
as her body ping-ponged with pheromones.
Pews empty as an abandoned grandstand,
there she stayed for awhile—feeling at odds.

O the Curse of Eve—Original Sin;
God, that time again, the painters are in.

25. *cities are whorehouses*

Floating about on a boat at night feels
like you're moving almost as fast as stars,
moonlight skimming over riverine trash,
lurid sunsets raw as a throat red gash.
Strewn along river banks the hulks of cars,
currents coiling sluggish, oily as eels.
Throughout the countryside, things fall to bits,
spotted with lazy housing and pre-fabs.
Cities are whorehouses, small towns, kennels;
she fancied teaching abroad, cheap rentals,
so googled to see what was up for grabs,
then checked out Asia, and got a few hits.

Like a dream it felt all too far away,
such murky visions—she felt quite distrait.

26. *Headlands Hotel*

Disorientation. Which path to take?
She considered east and west, north or south;
magnetic compass faltered, thoughts turned fog,
migratory birds through 'electro-smog.'
Her best option by far seemed word-of-mouth,
glossy package deals, she dismissed as fake.
The family packed up off to Thirroul
for Christmas holidays on the south coast;
but those memories lay drowned in sea mist.
The Headlands Hotel where she first got pissed,
the surfers and barbies, the Sunday roast—
that mad New Year when she near lost it all …

Coal carriers—troubling the horizon,
black and massive, the line lifted, broken.

27. *an inch of daylight*

Hair scattered carelessly about her neck,
nails painted reflective as champagne flutes.
She liked him as he came across so calm,
she trusted him because he meant no harm
that 'copter gun-ship guy in army boots,
said he'd done a tour or two—in Iraq.
 'Let's drink! Why are we waiting for the lamps?'
and then, pointing to his first finger joint,
guffawed, 'Only an inch of daylight left.'
He quoted old Greek poets as the best,
warrior words sharp as any spear point;
sung with a lyre around those tented camps.

Alcaeus, in his storm-tossed ship praying
that St. Elmo's Fire—frap mast and rigging.

28. *scattered husks*

Well, life didn't overly trouble her,
the bleary light bristled, horizon wide.
An overarching, harbour bridge rose grey
under the persistent, pagan blue sky.
She saw earthly shadow and moon collide,
and soft as ash, the day became a blur.
She concluded that beauty lay in mime;
no sooner done than lost as afterthought.
You cannot step twice into the same stream,
everything begins and ends in a dream.
The scattered husks of history are naught,
or whatever else shifts the hands of time.

If life proved to be nothing but a farce,
on balance—she didn't give a rat's arse.

29. *an oyster shell galaxy*

She sensed time into oblivion slide,
pearls, within an oyster shell galaxy,
and feathered light that from its edges fell.
Curdy clouds somersaulted by pell-mell
over harbour and mountaintops spiky,
on palms along the length of the quayside.
Emerged a yellow sandstone cathedral
with narrow, humid streets leading to it;
monumental—once a pagan fortress.
Boys in ruffles and girls in baroque dress;
a procession at dusk, slow, elegant
as bas-relief carved on some pedestal.

The town felt empty, the people remote,
she turned as if about to speak, and woke.

30. *the promise of falsehood*

What memory, skin—left by a lover,
fingerprints (imprisoned) clear as tree bark;
and what remains of the intimate sigh?
She sought the promise of falsehood—the lie,
protection against the truth as bulwark.
She chose to believe when it was over
by keeping her distance she kept the view.
One step ahead of herself, and one back,
a race run according to her own pace.
Socially, that meant she never lost face
and shuffled her suitors like a card pack,
is how she played it though lovers were few.

Does love shift the heart to another gear?
Her visage in the mirror prismed a tear.

31. *half stonkered*

How many heroes were alcoholics?
Most who partied big time in the mead halls
fired themselves up and into battle went;
courageous, until the body flagged, spent.
Lovemaking comes with its own set of rules,
alcohol makes for brave bedroom frolics.
Alexander, now there was a pisspot,
who, hungover, many nations conquered—
and then assumed the role of demigod.
That's what did for him in the end, poor sod,
the Macedonian was half stonkered!
The grave as empire, that became his lot.

Queried about his drinking days, he said,
'All booze does is make a hole in the head.'

32. *Hellenic Bakery*

Down Illawarra then by Wemyss Street,
across Addison and Sydenham Road,
past brick villas with Dahlia gardens
(the first settled Greeks and Italians)
across the iron railway bridge she strode
munching an Hellenic Bakery treat.
As clouds built big airy tents overhead
she passed by a butcher and barber shop,
stepping over many a trachyte kerb.
Globule cut across Marrickville suburb—
at the cycleway she came to a stop,
so veered off to the Cooks River instead.

The river crawled under a pumice sky,
a bunch of office joggers bounced on by.

33. *takes all sorts*

Wasn't her idea of New York City—
crossdressers, ladyboys, traps, transvestites,
hustling blowjobs down on 12th Avenue.
Dudes traveling across from Jersey through
the Lincoln Tunnel for sex, boogie nights
in the meat packing district of Chelsea.
But hey, the Big City, it takes all sorts;
Sydney is no slouch when it comes to sleaze,
it teaches a girl how to pick her mark;
nailing some suit—just a walk in the park.
It's no easy thing for women to please,
to put on a game face, and be good sports.

We give thanks to the city's soothsayers,
cabbies, concierges, and bartenders.

34. *'with unhurrying chase'*

Globule looked into the silvery glass,
ghostly figures flitted across her screen
appeared and disappeared in a flicker.
The days felt grainy, the hours grew thicker.
Moonrise, full and bold as any stop sign;
'Vertigo,' she thought, 'surely it would pass.'
As if she had become another self;
one hidden behind her own reflection,
who played hide and seek within the mirror.
Someone like her, though not as *de rigueur*,
as if reason gave way, past detection,
with 'unhurrying chase', taken by stealth.

A *folie à deux*—the mirror complied,
Maslow's basic needs well within her stride.

35. *outside of time*

Her head an empty, off-season resort,
nothing but the dumb echo of her heart;
memory fluttered, one tattered, silk scarf.
Yearning, an ever-diminishing path—
wind shuffled the sky's installation art
and the moon bustled yellow as bellwort.
She felt oddly displaced, outside of time,
a mass of protons that could not survive
this open-ended wormhole we call life;
what future promised anything but strife?
Yet if the shattered self did not revive,
she pursued fossil light back to its prime.

Stars remind us death is not a blank wall,
that gravity happened after The Fall.

36. *Jesus hobo*

A minimalist artist planned to paint
CityRail—call it, 'Stations of the Cross'
(the line ran from the city to the coast):
a Lee Marvin type Jesus hobo ghost
with Ernest Borgnine as the rail-guard boss;
one fierce duel between devil and saint.
Every good story has one girl in it—
but how to paint Mary Magdalene's face?
Surely, the most human of heroines;
compassionate, for all her supposed sins.
One who plied her trade in the marketplace,
but she was destined to become prophet.

At death—the spirit repeats its journey,
seeks again and again some new body.

37. *nereid of the waves*

Interlocking mortise and tenon cloud:
steadily, that sky unscrolls its blueprint—
she, the companion to light, shape-shifter,
dreams herself as waterspout and twister
dancing up the harbour in merriment,
who sways louchely as a watery shroud.
Undine or sprite—nereid of the waves,
a woman who would suffocate a man,
capture his breath with a kiss if betrayed;
does true love exist beyond getting laid?
One night stands—no, she was never a fan,
though, occasionally, one misbehaves.

Sydney girls, obsessed with real estate,
ensnare your man, get your house, renovate!

38. *that which haunts*

How much anyone knows or not is all
about perspectives, tallying the loss.
Those troubled vistas of broken statues,
marble painted in reds or smoky hues
wrought under a bronze sky gone verdigris,
and the heart's barricades about to fall.
The two selves billeted within one breast,
eidetic memory, and that which haunts
within the amphitheatre of the mind—
what one will forget, the other will find,
which of these is it that teases or taunts
the workings of a heart that cannot rest?

In the alpine valley the dam wall burst,
you weren't in love, just perfectly rehearsed.

39. *a dream of Sorrento*

'On the hotel terrace facing the sea'
what do you envisage, hearing that phrase,
sunlight on blue waters, but is this all?
Boredom or sex, a Graham Greene novel;
an horizon that blurs into sea haze,
the shock-still silhouette of one palm tree.
The movie star fidgets with his cufflinks—
though today, he will play the dictator,
resplendent in his braided uniform;
clouds mass to purple, the gathering storm.
Poolside, the leading lady sips vodka,
between takes one of her favourite drinks.

A dream of Sorrento, Bay of Naples,
tanks move into the plaza, then night falls.

40. *egalité*

Is she Maid Marian or Mockingjay:
do old heroines dream us, and we them?
Some supercharged, armour-clad, ultra fem,
some chic Joan of Arc for egalité.
A sunset strewn across the windowpane
as the Camel Lady trekked through her dreams.
Scimitar curve of shadow off sand dunes
as her thoughts swung onto the passing lane.
But lodged at the back of every girl's mind
lies the worldly Eve, the Magdalena,
who taught that spirit is born of trauma—
her teachings usurped, her image maligned.

The heartbeat repeats its troubled motif,
loneliness is another name for grief.

41. *crimson bruise*

Victoria State ablaze with bushfires,
destruction along the Great Ocean Road;
Separation Creek, Wye River, houses,
properties, livestock—cinders and ashes;
the Otway Ranges ready to implode ...
street after street reduced to smoking pyres.
This is the Australian bushfire season:
'today's expected high will reach forty'
as sunsets expand in a crimson bruise
from the Blue Mountains out to La Perouse.
Flaming pennants, an advancing army,
every state braced against the invasion.

Sitting on a balcony in Newtown,
around her sooty embers fluttered down.

42. *Olympia Milk Bar*

Walking by the Olympia Milk Bar
(over there the Stanmore Cinema stood),
interior a dark, chthonic grotto—
everything faded like an old photo,
little survives of the old neighbourhood;
Mr Fotiou lives here, the Greek owner.
50s advert signs drearily displayed:
'ice cream sodas' and 'time for a Kit Kat.'
Bold gold letters, 'Olympia Salon,'
'style cutting' and 'perms' a faded icon.
His wife dying terminated all that;
he dreams her dancing in a forest glade.

A skateboarder clatters by, traffic hums,
Mr Fotiou sweeps his floor, no one comes.

43. *this harlot saint*

Mary Magdalene sailed from Judea
in a rudderless boat—banished—to die,
with a few disciples, the story goes;
arriving at Marseille, how no one knows,
became a hermit in Provence, no lie,
made it big in France, this saintly sinner.
St. Baume grotto and St Maximin Church,
hot ticket items on the pilgrim route.
Cinnamon, myrrh, aromatic face paint,
no pop diva could match this harlot saint;
and then Jesus threw seven devils out,
O the hawk never flies far from the perch.

Women pray for a man's unselfish love,
right here on earth—not in heaven above.

44. *act of defiance*

At first, you imagined a boulevard,
the afternoon cool, had it been raining?
That giddy sense of anticipation
under a greyish sky and wintry sun.
You recollected that Paris street scene—
a photograph captured on a postcard;
Doisneau's—Le Baiser de l'hôtel de ville.
Here is love as an act of defiance,
the city breathing, free, yet newly born.
But what resides at the heart of the storm
may prove passion a fragile alliance;
for these lovers time forever stands still.

In the backstreets of the city somewhere,
one plain fountain in an abandoned square.

45. Mt. Athos

So she sat frozen before the portrait
in the gallery, grotesque as it was,
the painting looked at her, and she at it,
a frame of reference, the perfect fit;
Germaine Greer sculpted onto Mt Athos,
a ball-breaking, post-feminist piss-take.
One hand clenched tight in salute as a fist,
the other cupped the City of Sydney.
Allegory, island of the mind, farce,
Mt Athos trembled under the great arse.
Her face as blank as a monastery,
a monstrous dildo tethered to the wrist.

A thought floated up inside Globule's head,
'how can you be desperate if you're dead.'

46. *before shunters*

Rookwood Cemetery tracks to Regent
Street, Mortuary Station, Chippendale,
a stone's throw from Central Railway Station,
the dead transported in slow procession.
The dead don't complain, are beyond the pale,
the dead don't hurry, the dead are patient.
Architecture claims the high moral ground:
this sandstone structure rolls with the punches,
its crimson and yellow bands transmitting
light, North to South, a million grains glinting.
Close by, carriages bunch before shunters,
then someone shouts the office crew a round.

She says, there can never be another,
but she knows that nothing lasts forever.

47. *so long*

Probert St, the most burgled in Sydney,
or was, according to local folklore;
pot plants got stolen if not bolted down.
The cheapest rentals to be had in town,
an old working-class suburb, but no more—
why lament the loss of what used to be?
A photo's a dream you've departed from,
become memory, a faded address.
Joy soon wanes dissolves into sentiment;
empty as any condemned tenement.
Bustling birdsong in volumes evanesce
down dusty country roads calling, so long.

Would she become a Mullumbimby chick,
bouncing some baby on her floral hip?

48. *O Sirius*

Brutalism! If I must with thee dwell
between opera house and harbour bridge ...
salutations, Sirius, in The Rocks,
each apartment a tidy concrete box.
Cosy, bigger than your average fridge—
'Demolish it!' I hear councillors yell.
Monument to the Green Bans, Millers Point,
public housing, the long term resident
harking back to sailing ships and steamers.
Sydney isn't a city for dreamers;
it's for investors, not the mendicant,
is memory-deprived, time out of joint.

High up on that building an SOS
sign flickers nightly: 'Save Our Sirius'.

49. Sophie Scholl

'Such a fine, sunny day, I have to leave …'
Sophie Scholl, anti-Nazi activist.
She was executed by guillotine
for standing up against Hitler's machine.
Twenty-one, Munich student, naturist;
the charge of high treason meant no reprieve.
Her executioner dressed formally:
black coat and gloves, a bow-tie and top-hat.
He was, of course, efficient at his job,
had entered 3,000 kills in his log.
Her head slid from her shoulders to the mat,
prison staff said she died with dignity.

Her namesake, that women from Judea,
Sophie Scholl's middle name, 'Magdalena'.

50. *hillock of her hip*

Aside from the yellow lit daffodils,
just weather, with a furrow on its brow.
If living is an act of postponement,
youth is the dream, the eternal moment.
Globule resided in the here and now,
a handful of dreams, a few basic skills;
she saw herself living inside a cave.
The sun sank on the hillock of her hip;
O for a shack on a hill and sea view,
Illawarra escarpment running through.
To escape the city, take a train trip,
meanwhile, a surfer rode another wave.

Who would die of a broken heart today
given the temptations put in our way?

51. *loop*

She halted under the Iron Cove Bridge,
pigeons on girders clattered noisily.
She felt the *whump* of traffic overhead,
deep quad stretches, a sun flexed rusty red.
Globule tackled the bay run twice weekly
looping from Leichardt back across the bridge.
Daylight lifted off the inner-harbour,
slid down between the sandstone abutments.
Shadow made of this a filtered grotto,
the moment captured, a smartphone foto.
Windows flashed off harbourside tenements,
traffic thickened—became an armada.

Jogged into Rozelle, hassled by some jerk
cruising in a chintzy, salmon pink Merc.

52. *bad mistake*

She'd come across them, unexpectedly,
though was headed toward Strawberry Hills.
Eveleigh Street through a lane to The Block,
shooting up on the curb, it was a shock.
Taken a shortcut—got lost—not for thrills,
what to do, turn back, or walk on boldly?
Slap bang into the middle of Redfern,
figures in doorways, she stared straight ahead;
had come out onto that infamous street—
bad mistake, skin prickly, heavy heartbeat,
her legs scissoring, but they felt like lead;
broken beer bottles, she smelt car tyres burn.

Recurrent ghastly dreams, embattled sleep,
'her veins had drunk the deadly poison deep.'

53. *generations*

Devils Marbles / the Tanami Desert,
the very air ignited sand to glass;
molten tear drops of some ancestral god.
Here, the Arrernte and Warlpiri trod
or tracked, and generations came to pass;
rocky terrain and small hills comprise it.
A mirage becomes a hovering lake;
does stillness in deserts suggest water,
a silence so profound it cries regret?
Of memory—the direction is set,
there, within the circle, hums forever;
nearby, the depot, though it was too late.

One derelict truck again proved the rule,
'never go bush without enough fuel.'

54. Thecla

Thecla followed Paul, rejected marriage:
'O blessèd are those who keep the flesh chaste,
for they shall become a temple of God.'
She bought it, but that didn't spare the rod;
'opposing nuptials' the charge Thecla faced,
she got the death sentence, a miscarriage.
The whole thing kicked off at Iconium;
first, the lit pyre a godly rain cloud doused,
then thrown to beasts, a lioness saved her;
women threw—amomum, nard, cassia,
perfumes hypnotized and the lions drowsed;
her beauty stunned all in that stadium.

Short of stature, man or angel, no fool,
bandy-legs and bald, a hooked nose, was Paul.

55. *never look back*

From Ovid, through Virgil, Sir Orfeo,
there are many who sing of Orpheus:
his doomed quest to retrieve Eurydice;
Lot's wife turned into salt by the Dead Sea.
Never look back, the past is perilous,
hero and fool's boneyard, a phantom show.
Desire not reciprocated twists love,
makes of it a lust and troubling regret.
We call forth the ghosts to kill off the guilt,
oblations were made and the temple built.
In some sleazy chat room the lovers met,
nothing came of it—if push came to shove.

The bucket clatters in the empty well,
to mourn lost love these days is a hard sell.

56 twilight bat

Artists departing in droves to 'The Gong',
Newcastle, Central Coast, Southern Highlands,
Sydney was always consumed by its greed.
The rampage of developers, on speed,
consuming neighbourly parks, such big plans;
hotels and apartment blocks, same old song.
Yet something of the old charm still remains;
rosella colour-banded sandstone walls,
chunky girdered rail bridges spanning streets.
Jacaranda laneways, twilight bat bleeps—
electrical storms and sudden rain squalls,
metallic screech and fade of Newtown trains.

Siren shriek from the depths of the city,
is this the ghost of Jackie Orszacsky?

57. *yet retain a hold*

Crass Meriton development (Sydney)
nailing down the coffin lid on the old,
raddled jack hammers ringing neighbourhoods;
self-serviced apartments with all the goods.
Still, a few backstreets yet retain a hold,
terraces, villas, the bottle brush tree…
Pocket handkerchief parks and squat brick walls,
balconies with ornate iron fretwork.
Refuse laden laneways and granny flats,
grey, wooden palings, ready to collapse—
the garrulous Greek and taciturn Turk,
the working-class pubs, the dim lit pool halls.

High walled presbytery, minus the Lord,
low plane roar over Chelmsford to Kingsford.

58. *tiny nails*

Alone, in a huge black top parking lot,
falling through aether—planet by planet,
her dream unravelled like a toilet roll;
'tiny nails' fastened her body to soul,
drawn into the five zones by earth's magnet:
but waking up was as far as she got.
Slam dunked in a relationship, it stopped,
like mid-sentence or half way through a smile;
as if an ancient voice had whispered, 'no!'
Her heart quick-slowed as a glacial flow;
as if she'd not been surprised in a while,
envisioned the past, so the penny dropped.

Childhood lived as it should be, without fear,
life seemed so simple, horror, lurked elsewhere.

59. techies and hipsters

O when Eve was Adam and Afterwards:
when trespass signs hung in all the forests
and each footstep proclaimed a holy shrine,
an eye blink the measure of each lifetime;
citizens of the New World, or tourists?
Abandoned creatures, no longer God's wards.
Language broke down in her skull, no worries!
Preferred bars full of techies and hipsters
as psychic songs played in her head, unheard.
A world endangered? It never occurred!
She used her sex to cull out the losers,
One night stands—usual flirt and flurries.

As to sexual hijinks, no question,
such hurdles were purely equestrian.

60. *slow blur*

Globule, trapped in a lift, talk about rude,
never read a book in his pointless life;
another Shane Warne dropkick sporting bling
who'd con some girl into a marriage ring,
a mouse-scared checkout chick born into strife
destined for this loser, this dumb arse dude.
Bragging to his even more stupid mate
about muscle cars, piss ups, backseat screws,
though his loud rant was directed at her.
Floor buttons counted down in a slow blur—
then she pushed past him muttering, 'excuse',
it felt like some weird dream and no escape.

Just another westie, yeehaw, redneck,
steel cap boots, navy singlet, trackies (check).

61. oikoumene

She cut across Callan Park to the bay,
discovered a sailing ship carved in rock
big as a dinner plate and weather smudged.
Some idle afternoon, a sailor trudged
up to The Point, rested maybe, took stock,
looked over to his ship on that bright day …
She sat, Iron Cove bristled in sunlight,
felt self-contained and content, yet alone—
just one more chick in a tank top texting.
A yacht at anchor, its lanyard rattling …
She dreamed herself a sibyl on her throne,
and fell into a trance, then she took flight.

What could she have possibly left behind,
but the closed *oikoumene* of her mind.

62. *passed her by*

In the cold snap of this dream a bushfire
rose and raged silent as some virus through
her veins, crowning the patter of her heart,
that pulse of flame, and woke her with a start—
out of ash cloud a Pied Currawong flew;
Globule had dreamed her bed a burning pyre.
Leapt up into the sky, then clean through it,
disappeared down a wormhole, forever;
one panpsychistic comet passed her by. . .
Do what your Pa said, keep your powder dry;
she got up then got her shit together,
do what your Ma told, and shoot from the hip.

Globule found an old book called Heroides,
she'd given up finding a man to please.

63. *hearts that harden*

She sat in the Warren View beer garden
beneath the frangipani tree—Ovid
on table, and of the many versions,
she settled on Clare Pollard's 'Heroines'.
Women writing warriors, she loved it,
read of hearts that bled and hearts that harden.
How Phyllis turned into an almond tree
that bloomed as her lover clasped it in grief;
or elms that grew from Protesilaus' tomb—
top leaves in sight of Troy withered in gloom.
Sitting there in the shade she felt relief,
emboldened even, though, somehow wary.

Once, it was looking ahead, now it's back,
had she now found herself on the right track?

64. Penelope to Ulysses / i

So it is, Troy has fallen, where are you?
O that Paris had drowned in a sea storm—
I wouldn't be in this perilous state
stalked by drunk predators who party late,
as I hide away locked up in my room;
I repel them with guile, how I miss you!
When I heard who in the Argive camp fell,
I feared for you, the blood in my veins froze.
Where Troy stood acres of barley rustle,
warriors that swung sword now swing sickle.
Word from Sparta or Pylos? No one knows;
maybe a slut has your heart, who can tell.

I pray for your return, yet I falter,
your son, Telemachus, needs his father.

65. Phyllis to Demophoon / ii

Those of us who truly love count the days,
pray our beloved returns to us soon;
we cannot believe in that which gives hurt.
You seduced me with lies, left me inert,
swore that you'd return by the next full moon;
daily, to the horizon, turn my gaze ...
wind-scuffed sea, seeking your sail, only cloud.
Brutal man! You used and abandoned me,
your promises to the gods all an act
to draw me to your arms, we had a pact.
Empty words and false tears, what gallantry!
My bright vision of you is now my shroud.

Two-faced guest of my Thracian estate,
sea squalls, foamy rocks, cry out—and I wait.

66. *Briseis to Achilles / iii*

I write tearful words, I fear it's too late,
you handed me over to men the king
sent without so much as one farewell kiss.
Captive a second time, O my distress
at leaving—saw my family dying
by your hand, again, thus sealing my fate!
You sulk within your tent, refuse battle.
If Agamemnon offers you treasure,
tripods and gold, Lesbos girls, my return,
you hesitate, are slow to anger, spurn
all entreaties—is this your love's measure,
am I nothing more to you than chattel?

I never slept with the Mycenaean,
Achilles! My love defines who I am.

67. *Phaedra to Hippolytus / iv*

If love comes to me late it enters deep.
My words falter before you, my heart quakes,
lips tremble, my body hungers for yours;
where passion is concerned there are few laws,
to have you—I'll do whatever it takes;
I ache, can only have you in my sleep.
Strangely, to seek wild beasts, I am driven,
in forests to net deer, hounds to the ridge,
spear cast, lay my body on grassy ground.
With what skill you circle your horse around,
madness in my blood takes me to the edge;
Theseus' crimes will not be forgiven.

Our love will look normal, not out of line,
Jove states that what gives us pleasure is fine.

68. Oenone to Paris / v

So what if I slut-shamed whorish Helen,
for as you took her she took you from me.
By the sacred fountains of Mount Ida,
I warned you, do not hoist sail for Sparta,
even so, shipwrights felled the thick fir tree;
believe it, you are your own destruction.
Shepherd prince of noble birth wanting more
tossed me aside like some dirty dish rag,
for that rich bitch who ditched Menelaus;
chaos and death await you, I see this!
My love given is true, not like that slag—
you will return after wading through gore.

You beg me to heal your wounds, I will not,
far as I'm concerned, Paris, you can rot!

69. Hypsipyle to Jason / vi

You completed what you set out to do—
sowed the serpent's teeth that grew an army,
yoked fire-breathing oxen to plough a field;
and then, to make the sleepless dragon yield,
drugged it, filched the golden fleece, sailed away;
taking that witch, Medea, back with you!
Back to Thessaly to reclaim your throne,
and yet, I've heard nothing from you, Jason;
are you bewitched, or is *Argo* becalmed,
that woman killed her brother, who else harmed?
I've given birth to twins from our union,
when your seed flooded me, recall my moan.

I'm as faithful to you as to Lemnos,
could Medea claim the same for Colchis?

70. *Dido to Aeneas / vii*

Go, depart, the uncoupling sea calls you,
inconstant lover who beached on these shores.
I brought you to safety behind wide walls,
honoured your person in glittering halls.
Carthage stands strong against threatening wars
yet my brother in Tyre wants me dead too.
As waves roll you forward on the long sea
and your wife's ghost guides you to the Tiber,
there to found a city upon its banks
and build a great army in serried ranks,
know me for the one who will remember;
recall then my touch, both faint and ghostly.

Aeneas, your fleet rides in the roadstead,
one last time you rough-handled me to bed.

71. *Hermione to Orestes / viii*

Pyrrhus tries to bully me into bed.
Did Menelaus mope in empty halls
when Paris whisked Helen away to Troy?
I don't want a thousand ships or army,
just you, Orestes, it is you who rules
my heart, none other, listen! I am scared.
Grandsire Tyndareus gave me to you,
but my father decided otherwise—
for Achilles' son, but it's you I love,
you're duty-bound to me, the gods above;
kill again for honour, I am your prize,
he will not have me as my heart is true.

My tears fed with anger, I am helpless,
will I fall victim to rape, regardless?

72. *Deianira to Hercules / ix*

O what fates I fashion for you my love,
wild boar and lion, serpents, hounds of hell.
Is it true you cross-dress, wear tranny bling,
that on command trill, in falsetto, sing?
I heard Omphale caught you in her spell,
the hand that held a club flaunts a kid glove.
The foe you defeated would laugh out loud,
to trumpet your twelve labours sounds hollow;
your manhood reduced to this mockery,
and now you've returned home with Iole—
I can't compete with her beauty I know;
the love-vest I gave you is now your shroud.

The world's safer because of those you smote,
yet Venus has her heel pressed to your throat.

73. *Ariadne to Theseus / x*

The surf, a frosty moon, birdcall, woke me,
turning to embrace your warmth I found none;
ship and crew, vanished on the horizon.
Frantic, this way and that, my heart frozen
I called your name, 'Theseus!' but felt numb,
climbed a hill, knotted my veil to a tree
to signal what I thought your full-blown sail,
but it was only some dissolving cloud—
you'd abandoned me in sleep, you had fled,
where we slept that last night, now a cold bed.
Alone, a bleak island, I cried out loud,
your heart's thread to mine cut, I felt mine fail.

Only the gulls, the screeching wind, sea-wrack,
I plunged hands into waves to pull you back.

74. *Canace to Macareus / xi*

In one hand, a pen, the other, a blade,
my missive is obscured by blood, not tears.
A barrage of wind blasts from Aeolus,
my child by you, dear brother, is my loss—
his grandson, ripped apart by wolves and bears,
abandoned in the woods, cold and afraid.
My nurse tried to safeguard me from the wrath
with babe hid in a basket, then as she
walked by the king the child cried out in fright,
our unhallowed love discovered that night.
Nowhere could I shelter from his fury;
our child exposed, Aeolus sought my death.

You would not marry me, Macareus,
find your son's bones and mix with my ashes.

75. *Medea to Jason / xii*

My magic protected, got you the fleece,
fiery bulls, snake fangs, a crop of wild men,
the dragon drugged yielded up the trophy;
a hard-won golden pelt was my dowry,
reminding you, gives me pleasure, Jason.
Betrayer! with a new wife on your leash,
her father's wealthy, but then, so too mine—
I am from Colchis, she is from Corinth;
King Creon's daughter, Creusa, your bride.
Now it's my company you can't abide,
would your heart grow fonder in my absence?
We were invincible, drank blood like wine.

So be it, banish me from your palace,
traitor! there are few bounds to my malice.

76. *Laodamia to Protesilaus / xiii*

My heart is shot through, Protesilaus,
you sailed away and took the light with you.
I reeled, fell to the floor in a dead faint,
Paris stole Helen, now war, is my plaint.
Those days the gods grant us are all too few—
beware Hector, against him you will lose;
Trojans, hear this plea, let my husband live
who is better suited to love than war.
Menelaus seeks his queen, it's his right,
husband, this is not your quarrel, why fight?
I pray you're not the first to step ashore,
prophecy states that soldier won't survive.

Your ship the first to beach is what I fear,
as you stepped, the flash of the Dardan spear.

77. *Hypermnestra to Lynceus / xiv*

Forty-nine brides each guilty of murder,
that I held back, refused to slash your throat
was my crime—I disobeyed Danaus—
our wedding night, greasy smoke of torches;
a feast of meat and wine designed to bloat,
lull the grooms into a drunken stupor.
Three times I raised my blade over your head,
the dagger traced your throat, no! I could not.
Debated with self, but did not kill you;
your brothers' dying screams I heard, it's true.
I woke you, fiercely whispered of the plot,
'brothers, all dead, Lynceus—flee!' I said.

Here I languish, prone on the prison floor,
my wrists are shackled, I can write no more.

78. *Sappho to Phaon / xv*

If my lines tumble, do you wonder why?
Sappho is world-famous for her lyric
celebrating bright-eyed girls of these lands,
crowned with violet, dill woven garlands.
Should lust win out—the victory's pyrrhic,
the lyre weaves songs of love not elegy.
My wine-trading, whore-mongering brother
hates me also, it seems, for honest talk.
You too, Phaon? I speak truth about this;
you are gone, I am dumb—it's you I miss.
I've haunted forests that hosted our sport,
nothing but cold earth, it makes me shudder.

Turn your craft about, I mean you no harm,
great squalls—usually followed by calm.

79. *no oracles*

O Heroides! Murder. Fratricide. War!
Her scene suddenly felt selfish and mean,
petty concerns offered little appeal.
These hero women, imagined—real,
believed that to betray love was obscene;
a heart so treated will settle the score.
Social media. Instagram. Textspeak.
Alas—no oracles might be found there—
momentarily, time ceased, then silence;
all her senses sharpened to prescience.
She saw calmness assume the guise of fear
as the world slowly turned under her feet.

An afternoon observing how light spills,
footsteps of gods, cloud-shadow over hills.

80. *follow the rails*

Chasing recollections, atmospherics,
labyrinths of the mind, sudden and fleet,
those utopias that will not be found.
The hum in the head that emits no sound,
parallel lines in space that never meet.
Globule was done with city hysterics,
she'd decided to strike out for the coast …
travel north for awhile, follow the rails.
Waiting on the platform down at Central
she recalled her last trip to Newcastle—
coal carriers lined up, bulky as whales,
one pelican, hanging, pale as a ghost.

Someone's radio exhaled an old song,
'the last train out of Sydney's almost gone.'

NOTES

THE SONG OF GLOBULE, a play of consciousness, owes something to John Gallas' jaunty sonnet sequence *The Story of Molecule* (Carcanet). All those shield clashing, Anglo Saxon consonants banging away happily together. An engaging take on what might be seen as an ontological 'Boys' Own' adventure set on the West Coast, South Island of New Zealand. These 80 sonnets on the other hand pursue the oneiric preoccupations of a young female protagonist living in Sydney who, if not suffering from multiple personality disorder, is certainly a fantasist. Her sensibilities continuously informed by a chorus of legendary heroines, both real and mythological. See my rendering of Ovid's *Heroides* into 15 of these sonnets: Nos: 64-78. The following brief notes are designed to assist the reader in locating a few of the more arcane quotes and references. Sydney landmarks are mostly self-explanatory. For the more intrepid reader I suggest the print edition of Gregory's *Sydney and Blue Mountains Street Directory*, and for those who enjoy tumbling through the wormhole of the Internet to get a no less distorted perspective—Google Earth.

5. 'Hey True Blue'

The title is taken from a song by the Australian folksinger and songwriter, John Williamson. The lyrics boast an unabashed if sentimental celebration of the Australian 'mateship' ethos. The ghost of ANZAC rides again. The Sydney monorail was a single loop connecting Darling Harbour, Chinatown and the CBD. A grotesque iron clad caterpillar that made a nasty, sandpapery rasping sound as it slid in-between buildings; an ugly contraption that added nothing to an already congested cityscape. One felt distinctly at risk while it passed asthmatically overhead. The mono-rail opened in July 1988 and closed in June 2013.

8. passed by a billboard

Sydney City Rail was known affectionately for its 'red rattlers'. Carriages painted a dull, faded red and rather dilapidated. They shook, rattled and rolled from one station to the next, and rarely if ever ran on time. 'The red rattler blitzes yet another appointment', was a common enough expression. In 1992 after 60 years of service the trains were finally retired.

Barons Tavern an infamous bar and a Kings Cross institution. In the mid-to-late 80s I spent time in this twilight zone doing a crash course in Sydney hedonism. The place closed down around 2007. The building was given over to luxury developers and subsequently demolished. The end of an era. Globule it must be remembered is a shape-shifter who glides seamlessly between past, present and future.

19. ceiling fans susurrated

'she gone with the man in the long black coat' from Bob Dylan's 'Oh Mercy' album (1989), which in this poet's opinion ranks with his best.

20. primal gardens

'for where the mind is there is the treasure' taken from the Gnostic text: *The Gospel According to Mary Magdalene*: Ch. 5:9: 'Blessed are you that you did not waver at the sight of me. For where the mind is there is the treasure.'

23. mickey finned

'O solitude! If I must with thee dwell,' title and first line of a sonnet by John Keats. How our perspective on what passes for reality alters over the centuries. Keats dreamed of quietude and the soul at peace; this same sonnet now might be seen as a lament for the destruction of the planet's wildernesses.

24. womby vaultage

The term suggests hollow recesses: a cave, womb or cupola, while 'return your mock / in second accent' implies an empty echo; thus a barren or futile exhortation to an authority figure or God—from: Henry V Act 2 Scene 3 by William Shakespeare.

> 'That caves and womby vaultages of France
> Shall chide your trespass and return your mock
> In second accent of his ordnance.'

27. an inch of daylight

The two quotes, 'Let's drink! Why are we waiting for the lamps?' And, 'Only an inch of daylight left', belong to the poet Alcaeus, native of Mytilene, Lesbos. He was born c. 620 BC and like his more famous contemporary, Sappho, with whom he may have had an affair; only fragments of his work survive as is the case with other Classical Greeks quoted here.

28. scattered husks

'You cannot step twice into the same stream'—famous quote from the Pre-Socratic philosopher, Herakleitos. He lived in Ephesus between 540 and 480 BC. 'The astuteness and comprehensiveness of his insight into the order of nature have commanded attention for 2500 years ... Plato counted him among the transcendent intelligences.' Taken from the Introduction: 7 GREEKS / Translations by Guy Davenport. A New Directions Book, 1995.

Reading, for me, is an act of transformation, not an exercise in rote, or compilation of authors read. It is not a list. 'Deep reading' is where the reader takes a given set of perceptions from a text - story, myth, or fact, etc, and remakes it, fashions what is read into his or her own perceptual image. Thus, to read is to make anew; it is an act of individual creation.

31. half stonkered

'All booze does is make a hole in the head.' Of course, it was not Alexander the Great (alcoholic) who said this, but that other great Macedonian warrior, and once renowned imbiber, the poet, James K. Baxter—or words to that effect.

32. Hellenic Bakery

Trachyte (*microsyenite*) is a dense igneous rock the equal of granite mined from Mount Gibraltar ('The Gib') quarries at Bowral from 1880 to 1986. It was used to replace Sydney's crumbling sandstone kerbs and gutters, and extensively used as dimension stone on major city buildings—many Heritage listed, for instance, Challis House, Martin Place, National Mutual Building, George Street, QVB, George Street, ANZAC Memorial, Hyde Park. Bowral Trachyte was used for major public works (Hawkesbury River Bridge at Brooklyn), and as commemorative stones for Federation and war memorials. A publication has been produced on the subject: 'Sydney's Hard Rock Story: The Cultural Heritage of Trachyte by Robert Irving, Ron Powell and Noel Irving. Leura, NSW. Heritage Publishing, 2014.

34. 'with unhurrying chase'

The title is a quote from Francis Thompson's haunted and unrelenting poem, *The Hound of Heaven*. 'Maslow's basic needs,'— *hierarchy of needs* was a theory put forward by the American Psychologist, Abraham Maslow (1908-1970). He emphasized the positive aspects of personality in order to help people realize their full potential.

36. Jesus hobo

Lee Marvin / Ernest Borgnine: *Emperor of the North* (1973). The movie is set in 1930s Depression America. The train jumping (Marvin) outwits the sadistic rail guard (Borgnine) who delights in knocking hobos off his goods train at high speed. The line, 'others saw her as chosen, the prophet' refers to the 2nd Century CE Gnostic text *The Gospel of Mary Magdala* (only fragments survive) in which Mary Magdalene is revealed as the first woman apostle. I see her as the embodiment of the sensual-erotic and the earthly sublime. *Das Ewig-Weibliche* ('the eternal feminine'—Goethe). A reverberative archetype deprived, I hasten to add, of its pedestal!

'At death the spirit repeats its journey / seeks again and again some new body.' Ancient Celts believed in the Pythagorean/Orphic *transmigration of souls* into the bodies of animals—spelt out in the dreamy neon lettering of the word: *metempsychosis*. North American Indian cosmologies, for example, hold that everything possesses a spirit that returns again and again in a new body. See: *Narrow Road to the Deep North* by Katherine McNamara, Mercury House, San Francisco, 2001.

38. *that which haunts*

'The two selves that beat within one breast,'. Gérard de Nerval in *Aurélia* states, 'I had a terrible idea. Every man has a double. I feel two men in myself.' Nerval was no doubt referring to the now famous quote from Goethe's Faust, *Zwei Seelen wohnen, ach! in meiner Brust*; translated as: *'Two souls, alas, are dwelling in my breast.'* Consciousness is the dialogue between Self and the Other. A double-sided mirror through which we pass toward and away from divergent points of existence. This has nothing to do with the notion of 'past lives' but belongs to the cyclical present. The mind plays compass by which we attempt to locate multifarious states of selfhood though, for most of us, what is disclosed is little more than simulacra.

39. a dream of Sorrento

'On the hotel terrace facing the sea' taken from Hans Magnus Enzenberger's epic poem, *The Sinking of The Titanic*, Ninth Canto. Did Globule visit the *Hotel Sorrento* on Mornington Peninsula, Melbourne, or dream of its namesake on the Amalfi coast? Had this been the case, we should certainly have heard.

40. egalité

Mockingjay is the last installment in the *Hunger Games* franchise starring *Jennifer Lawrence*, heroine in a dystopian world armed with her trusty bow and arrows and girl-next-door wholesomeness. Puzzling honesty before the surround-sound of danger every time. The human psyche rejoices in creating grandiose narratives that memorialize technological excesses on a doom-laden planet called earth. If we can pass the buck off as Sci Fi fantasy we can delude ourselves into believing that we have a little more breathing space left in a world rapidly running out of breath.

Camel Lady. The name given to Robyn Davidson who, in 1977 trekked 1,700 miles across the deserts of west Australia with camels as her sole means of transport. Her 'impossible' journey took nine months to complete. She wrote a book about these experiences called *Tracks*. 2013 saw the release of *Tracks* the movie directed by John Curran and starring *Mia Wasikowska* as Robyn Davidson in the lead role. Mandy Walker won the 2014 Best Cinematography award for *Tracks* from the Australian Cinematographers Society and the Film Critics Circle of Australia.

42. Olympia Milk Bar

The Olympia Milk Bar on Parramatta Road, Stanmore, hasn't changed in fifty years. The place is a time capsule, though more a shrine to the memory of Mr Nicholas Fotiou's dead wife than anything else. A mausoleum. The few tables remain eternally unoccupied. I did venture into this twilight zone once out of curiosity. No one to be seen. Once my eyes grew accustomed to the gloom, Mr Fotiou emerged from the shadows at the back of the shop into the crepuscular light like some sort of *Nosferatu* figure. He regarded me with a certain malice, but maybe his corpse-pale visage just gave that impression. I exchanged a few words about what, I can't recall exactly—his response was monosyllabic, sardonic even. A sad, haunted figure, lost to his memories, and probably a little crazy into the bargain. The Olympia Milk Bar was closed by order of the Inner West Council in November 2017 as, debatably, a threat to public safety. The building requires extensive repairs to its ceiling and facade. It cannot be demolished as it is listed on the NSW Heritage Register. Mr Fotiou has owned the milk bar since 1959. It is his life.

43. this harlot saint

Oscillating in gravitational waves throughout these sonnets might be detected the gnostic presence of *Mary Magdalene, Mary of Magdala*, also known as *The Magdalene*. St Baume Basilica at the foot of the Sainte-Baume Mountains in Aix-en-Provence is dedicated to Mary Magdalene where according to legend, she spent thirty years as a hermit in the caves there; an embellishment probably borrowed from the Greek legend of the reformed prostitute *Mary of Egypt* who lived in the 5th Century. Apparently, she became a prostitute at age twelve but, after converting to Christianity, spent the remainder of her years in the wilderness. The nearby monastery of St Maximin once claimed to be the original burial place of M.M. One of the more intriguing depictions of *Mary of Egypt* can be found in the short story by Honoré de Balzac, *The Unknown Masterpiece* (1831). See also: *Harlots of the Desert—A Study of Repentance in Early Monastic Sources* by Benedicta Ward, Cistercian Publications, 1987.

The American Queen of Bluegrass, Alison Krauss, stated in a television interview that every woman wants the 'unselfish love of a man' and that even as a child, whether she knows it or not, this is what she seeks. Between the dream and the fulfilment lies the stuff of legend—so we write poems and songs about the El Dorado of the Heart.

44. *act of defiance*

'Doisneau's—Le Baiser de l'hôtel de ville' needs little introduction and has stood as romantic emblem for *The City of Light* since first published in *Life* magazine, June 1950. For me this famous image reproduced on scores of posters and postcards over the years stands for something beyond romance, as an abiding symbol for the heroic spirit of Paris that cannot be defeated by the barbarians at the gate in any age. Robert Doisneau, French photographer (1912-1994). 'In the backstreets of the city …' During my brief visit to Paris back in 1979 I stayed not far from the Pompidou Centre on the Rue Notre Dame de Nazareth. One day I came upon a small square and fountain in the back streets. An impression of worn, grey stone. Low lying, nondescript apartments enclosed the square on all sides. Perhaps some wandering scholar or *vagante* passed this way once after a night of revelry and poetry at some grand house nearby. The place felt solitary, abandoned. There was no one to be seen. Hanging limply down over the broad rim of the fountain, *something*—was it a child's toy? Looking back, I can't be certain.

45. *Mt. Athos*

Dinocrates was Alexander the Great's leading architect who had pitched to the Macedonian that he sculpt Mt Athos, on the peninsula in north eastern Greece, in his likeness with a city in one hand and a bowl receiving all the rivers in the other. A grand and impossible dream depicted by many classical artists. This may have been the inspiration behind Gutzon Borglum's

Mount Rushmore sculptures. See *Landscape and Memory* by Simon Schama for more on this. Alexander pointed out that there would be insufficient land for the planting of grain to feed the populace. He instead tasked Dinocrates with designing the city of Alexandria. Germaine Greer carved into Mt Athos is perhaps more surrealist nightmare than dream.

48. *O Sirius*

The 79 apartments in The Rocks (Millers Point), Sydney, known as the Sirius Building were designed by the architect, Theo (Tao) Gofers between 1978-9. This public housing building is considered Australia's finest example of the *Brutalist* architectural style, arranged as it is in step-like formation around a central column. It was originally built to re-house public tenants after a controversial redevelopment of the neighbourhood during the 60s and 70s. Sirius is the only high rise in The Rocks situated close enough to the Sydney Harbour Bridge to appear almost within arm's reach. The residents fought to remain in the area and were supported by the Unions of the day in the celebrated Green Bans set up to preserve the heritage, architecture and public spaces of the community. In 2016 the Government of NSW denied the building Heritage listing and planned to demolish Sirius and replace it with a high-rise apartment block for the wealthy. This ruling was subsequently overturned and the building is now to be refurbished.

The reference to the SOS neon sign flashing from an upper story apartment relates to the *Save Our Sirius Foundation* supported by National Trust, the Australian Institute of Architects, the Millers Point Residents Action Group, Friends of Millers Point, Millers Point Public Housing Tenants Group, Unions NSW, and other sympathetic parties.

49. Sophie Scholl

Sophia Magdalena Scholl (1921-1943) was a German anti-Nazi political activist who belonged to the *White Rose*, a non-violent resistance group in Nazi Germany. She was convicted on a charge of high treason for distributing leaflets critical of Hitler at Munich University where she attended as a student at the time. She was executed by guillotine, along with her bother, Hans, also a member of the *White Rose*, for peaceful anti-Nazi activities on February 22, 1943, the same day as her conviction and death sentence. Sophie Scholl is today acclaimed a national hero for her courage in standing up against the Nazi war machine—she has been called a 'latter-day Joan of Arc.'

52. bad mistake

This incident actually happened to the author. I lived in a block of flats at 85 Chelmsford Street, Inner West, Newtown, Sydney. From my balcony on the first floor I overlooked Kent Lane to St Joseph's School and the presbytery referred to in *16. the enclosed garden* and *57. yet retain a hold*. I had that studio flat for seven years from Christmas 1986 (the year I arrived from NZ) through to 1992. I discovered years later that the poet, Henry Kendall (1839-1882), had resided at 124 Chelmsford Street when his first book, *Poems and Songs*, was published in 1862. I had not been the first, after all.

Regardless, I regularly walked down Cleveland Street off City Road to check my post office box located in Strawberry Hills; or alternately, veered off into Abercrombie St from the crest of King Street, as I did on this occasion. On a whim, I cut through Caroline lane which I thought might be a short cut, but ended at the top of Eveleigh Street, Redfern. In the laneway I ran into a bunch of smack freaks just after the dealer had arrived, a few sitting on the curb, while others had commandeered a vacant garage nearby—all shooting up. There must have been at least twenty junkies strewn about. No one appeared to even notice me, or so it seemed. I sort of freaked and walked stoically on, feigning a deadpan expression. I reckoned that to turn back and flee would alert them to my panic and I would be the worse off for it. I strode manfully on down the middle of Eveleigh Street through to Cleveland, swinging my arms, looking neither left nor right as if I owned the place, probably appearing quite deranged, and figuring that a display of bizarre confidence was far better than cringingly hoping to sidle out of the block unnoticed. The last line of the sonnet, 'her veins had drunk the deadly poison deep' is taken from Horace: Ode (1. xxvii).

53. *generations*

'the very air ignited sand to glass;' found in the Tanami Desert, west of Karlu Karlu (the Devils Marbles), the country of the Arrernte and Warlpiri. Apparently, this is seen as a relatively recent phenomenon, attributable to increased temperatures and climate change, where heated stones have caused the air to ignite, fusing sand to glass.

54. *Thecla*

Thecla was a devout follower of the Apostle Paul and his teachings, one of the earliest of the Christian women saints, who gained a strong cult following in the Middle Ages. Her legendary tale is contained in the *Acts of Paul and Thecla* written down around 150 AD. The legend itself probably came from earlier sources. The text accurately echoes the customs and traditional constraints of the times in which she supposedly lived. Nonetheless, early Christian women came to appreciate the ascetic practices suggested by the text, if that meant breaking from male-dominated marriages. Some things never change. The famous, and earliest known physical description of Paul (repeated in Classical paintings), is found in chapter one, verses four through seven of the extant text. Here is the description in full taken from 'The Acts of Paul and Thecla,' from *The Apocryphal New Testament*, translated by J.K. Elliott. Oxford University Press 1993. 'And he saw Paul coming, a man small in size, bald-headed, bandy-legged, of noble mien, with eyebrows meeting, rather hook-nosed, full of grace. Sometimes he seemed like a man, and sometimes he had the face of an angel.'

55. never look back

Arguably the closet comparisons to the *Orpheus and Eurydice* myth directly based on Ovid's *Metamorphoses* X-XII can be found in Virgil's *Georgics* IV, lines 453-527; Boethius' *The Consolation of Philosophy*, his poem at the close of Book 111; and the Breton lai, *Sir Orfeo*, a chivalric reworking of the Orpheus myth. I refer to the Tolkien translation of this anonymous, Middle English, Romantic poem.

56. twilight bat

An opinion piece in the *Sydney Morning Herald,* March 10, 2017 and headed up, 'I've always loved Sydney, but I'm starting to fear the marriage is over' by NZ born, Elizabeth Farrelly, who laments how Sydney has become too expensive for artists to live in anymore and who are leaving in droves. 'The scholars and poets and teachers exiled to woop-woop,' She then goes on to offer a warmed-over paean to the city's dwindling charms. 'There is still much to love; the pockets of sweetness and ancient need, moments when Sydney drops the hyper-shiny mask to reveal its true, damaged, brink-teetering self. The schizophrenic streets and sandstone kerbs, worn as teeth; the jazz dives and mahjong dens; the featherbeds six inches from the smack-soaked street, the horseback coppers and poetry bars and sudden gifts of poppies, the ferals and fetal alcohols, the rotten figs and drenching storms, the leafy eccentrics, the soup kitchens, the limping boys and bat-faced girls and rainforest acts of ludicrous kindness.'

Jackie Orszaczky was a Hungarian-born bandleader, composer, and musician extraordinaire central to the Sydney music scene for more than three decades. He played the Inner West at the Rose Hotel in Erskineville, for example, and the Newtown RSL where young musicians came to jam with Jackie on guitar. I recall seeing him languidly leaning back as he played off against all comers in a relaxed and friendly manner. I met Jackie briefly at the RSL and told him about an original music/poetry project that I was working on with fellow collaborator and friend, Matt Ottley, composer, picture book illustrator, that would eventually become a CD titled KING HIT (2007). He invited me to visit him at his residence but, regretfully, I never made it. Jackie died of lymphoma in 2008.

58. tiny nails

On the reference to 'tiny nails' and the 'five zones' see: *The Discarded Image* by C.S. Lewis, Cambridge University Press, 2016: pp: 60-61. Other references to ancient geography and the five zones go back to Parmenides, Aristotle and Cicero (The dream of Scipio) and others, through to Neoplatonism. References, for example, can be found in Virgil's *Georgics*, Book I: lines 231-56 and Ovid's *Metamorphoses*, Book 1: lines 45-51. The five zones feature in illustrated, Mediaeval zonal or 'wheel' maps defined as: the middle 'burning' zone (twice as wide as those listed here) and uninhabitable, two outer zones also uninhabitable because of extreme cold, the two temperate zones between the outer zones, the only habitable zones, especially the northern zone which constituted the then known world. The southern hemisphere or 'Terra incognita' was unreachable and its supposed antipodean inhabitants were fancifully and grotesquely depicted in Mediaeval Bestiaries. Today we might easily be persuaded that the 'burning' zone is rapidly widening as a result of climate change.

61. *oikoumene*

'but the closed *oikoumene* of her mind.' The term used by the Greeks throughout antiquity for the then known or inhabited world. 'The inhabited portion—the *oikoumene*—extended around the coasts of the Mediterranean and the Black Sea, and some distance into the interior.' Ref: Ancient Geography / The Discovery of The World in Classical Greece And Rome—Duane W. Roller. Published by I.B. Taurus, 2017. The toponyms that mark out the boundaries of Globule's mind are purely speculative.

•

A NOTE ABOUT THE AUTHOR

Stephen Oliver—Australasian poet and author of twenty volumes of poetry. Travelled extensively. Signed on with the radio ship *The Voice of Peace 1540 kHz* broadcasting in the Mediterranean out of Jaffa, Israel in the late 70s. Lived in Australia for 20 years. Currently living in NZ. He has published widely in international literary journals. Regular contributor of creative non-fiction and poems to *Antipodes: A Global Journal of Australian/New Zealand Literature*. Poems translated into German, Spanish, Chinese, and Russian. Represented most recently in the following: *Writing To The Wire Anthology*, edited by Dan Disney and Kit Kelen, University of Western Australia Publishing, 2016; *Manifesto: An Anthology of 101 Political Poems*, edited by Emma Neale and Philip Temple, OUP, 2017.

www.ingramcontent.com/pod-product-compliance
Lightning Source LLC
Chambersburg PA
CBHW030302010526
44107CB00053B/1781